Lonely Tony
A True Story

Mary Collins

Lonely Tony: A True Story, Published November, 2017

Editorial and proofreading services: Ashley Fedor; Karen Grennan
Interior layout and cover design: Howard Johnson
Interior and cover illustrations: Randy Jennings

All images inspired by Mia Hartwell's photos

SDP Publishing

Published by SDP Publishing, an imprint of SDP Publishing Solutions, LLC.

SDP Publishing
Permissions Department
PO Box 26
East Bridgewater, MA 02333
or email your request to info@SDPPublishing.com.

ISBN-13 (print): 978-0-9986730-6-6
ISBN-13 (ebook): 978-0-9986730-7-7

Printed in the United States of America

Dedication

To my grandchildren
and children of all ages
everywhere.

Acknowledgments

This book would not be possible without Mia Hartwell, John Hartwell, and Tony and Cleo.

I would also like to thank my publisher, Lisa Akoury-Ross of SDP Publishing, editor Ashley Fedor, illustrator Randy Jennings, and designer Howard Johnson.

Tony is the nickname of a boxer dog named Anthony. Tony had a sister named Cleo, short for Cleopatra. Together Anthony and Cleopatra were true Shakespearean characters. They lived near the beach in beautiful Massachusetts and had the best life together.

Tony loved the companionship of his sister Cleo. They were together every day, running on the beach, digging in the yard, and playing fetch.

"You are my best friend, Tony," said Cleo. Tony smiled.

"You are my best friend, too, Cleo," he replied.

But one sad day, Cleo got very sick, and within days she passed away, leaving Tony all alone. Tony missed Cleo very much.

Cleo was invited away to be with her Maker, God in heaven, and to receive her rewards for her kind life.

Tony knew this was so because of a story he had heard. Not too long ago, a little boy's pet dog died. This little boy, Angelo, lived in Rome, Italy. One day, Angelo met The Holy Father, Pope Francis. Angelo asked Francis if his dog was in heaven. Francis told Angelo, "We do not know that your pet is *not* in heaven."

Tony thought, "Now that Cleo has gone to heaven, I will have to make new friends."

Tony's owners, John and Mia, loved each other very much and liked doing things together. When they needed to make a visit to the local recycling center, they took Tony with them, because he was such good company.

At the Center was a llama named Leo. Tony had never seen anything like Leo before. Leo was very tall and fluffy, and had a sly smile.

"Hello, sir!" said Tony, walking up to the llama. "Would you be my friend?"

But Leo was too busy attending to the people dropping off their recycling, and didn't have time to talk to Tony. This made Tony sad. He knew he and the llama could be friends, if only the llama would take the time to look up and meet him.

Soon after, it was time for John and Mia to go to Winter Haven, Florida. The weather was getting cold up north, and the couple liked to spend the winter in the warmth down south. Of course, Tony went with them.

One afternoon a giant white egret named Gloria
flew by and saw Tony. She was called Gloria
because she was glorious, sparkling white. Tony
saw her while he was by a lake in Florida. He
approached Gloria cautiously. She was so beautiful
and graceful, it was almost as though she had come
down from heaven.

"Will you be my friend?" Tony asked the egret shyly.

"Yes, I would be happy to be your friend," Gloria replied graciously.

And so Gloria became Tony's first new friend. She would walk with him wherever he went. They loved to play catch, with Gloria gracefully tossing a frisbee for Tony to run after and retrieve.

In time, however, Gloria had duties she had to tend to and flew away.

Tony missed Gloria, and he especially still missed his Cleo every day. One morning, Tony was sitting in his yard when he heard a huge commotion. A big pig named Sassafras cracked through the picket fence to visit Tony. Sassafras was followed by a Chihuahua named Mexicana.

Mexicana kept her distance from Tony. He looked so big to her, and that made her afraid. However, Sassafras thought Tony was just the right size! So when Tony asked her, "Will you be my friend?" she said, "Yes!"

Sassafras liked Tony, as Gloria had.
Tony and Sassafras would take
walks together.

The owners of Sassafras and Mexicana came by to visit John and Mia. They said that Sassafras and Mexicana had to come with them, because it was time to head north.

And again Tony was alone.

Pam, John and Mia's daughter, came from Alabama to visit her parents in Florida. Pam had a chow-shepherd mix named T. Beau, who was a rescue dog. T. Beau and Tony had been pals for a long, long time.

"How are you doing, buddy?" T. Beau yelped when he saw Tony.

"Not so well," said Tony sadly. He explained to T. Beau that he was looking for a friend who wouldn't have to leave after a short time.

"Just keep looking and don't give up!" T. Beau encouraged Tony. "I know that someday you will be able to find a friend just like Cleo who won't have to go away."

Soon, Tony had another chance to make a new friend. John and Mia were heading to Ocala, Florida to visit friends. Of course, they took Tony.

Ocala is definitely horse country. In fact, Ocala was the home of Needles, the only Florida-bred horse to win the Kentucky Derby. Needles received his name because when he was little he had to frequently receive shots of medicine to cure a health problem. The shots worked, and Needles grew into a winner.

While Tony was in Ocala, he met a Clydesdale horse named Clyde.

Tony liked Clyde, and he was particularly pleased that they both had the same coloring. Tony asked Clyde if they could be friends.

"I would like to be friends, Tony. However, soon I have to go to a farm in St. Louis, one of the main homes of the Clydesdale horses," Clyde explained.

"Oh," said Tony, disappointed.

"Don't worry," said Clyde encouragingly. "I just know you will find a good friend soon!"

While in Ocala, John and Mia took Tony to an aquarium. Pam's niece, Alex, also went with them. There they met Al, a baby alligator. Alex enjoyed holding Al and kissing him. However, Tony had heard that alligators could run very fast. He didn't want to race with an alligator, so Tony just let Alex and Al be friends. "I definitely don't think Al will be my new buddy," Tony thought to himself.

After John, Mia, and Tony returned home from
Ocala to Winter Haven, a wonderful thing
happened. They were visited by two boxer puppies.

It was love at first sight. Tony knew these were the friends he had been searching for! But what should they be named? Tony had heard of a human boxer, an athlete. His name was Joe Louis. So Tony called one boxer puppy "Joe" and the other one "Louis."

Tony lovingly cared for the puppies. He showed them where their food was and when to eat. He also explained to them the need for good manners. This meant not begging for food at the table. A single "woof" by Tony was all that was needed if the puppies forgot.

Tony showed them where to sleep and tried the
bed first. The bed was not too little and not too big.
It was just right.

They frisked about and played dress-up. When they were in their red-white-and-blue, the dogs would romp and sing, "I'm a Yankee Doodle Dandy." Then they would howl with laughter and sing, "I'm a Yankee Doodle Boxer."

Tony was very happy. He looked forward to telling
Cleo about his adventures when they got together
again. Tony knew in his heart that Cleo was in heaven,
and one day he would see her there.

About the Author

Mary Collins, M.D. met Tony and Cleo while she was out for a walk. This led to her friendship with the dogs and their caretakers, John and Mia. Mary enjoys playing and reading with her grandchildren. She is a psychiatrist and lives in the Boston, Massachusetts area.

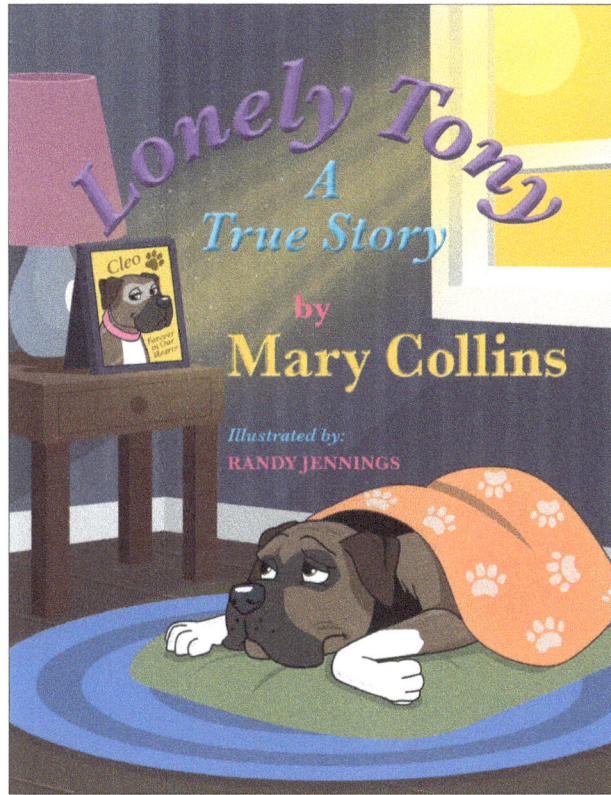

Lonely Tony *A True Story*
Mary Collins

Also available in ebook format

TO PURCHASE:
Available at all major bookstores

SDP Publishing

www.SDPPublishing.com

Contact us at: info@SDPPublishing.com